INSPIRATION FROM ENLIGHTENED NUNS

Susan Elbaum Jootla

BUDDHIST PUBLICATION SOCIETY
Kandy 1988 Sri Lanka

Buddhist Publication Society
P.O. Box 61
54, Sangharaja Mawatha
Kandy, Sri Lanka

ISBN 955-24-0032-5

Offset in Sri Lanka by
Karunaratna & Sons Ltd.
647, Kularatne Mawatha
Colombo 10

THE WHEEL PUBLICATION NO. 349/350

CONTENTS

INTRODUCTION

In this booklet we will be exploring poems composed by the Arahat bhikkhunis or enlightened Buddhist nuns of old, looking at these poems as springs of inspiration for contemporary Buddhists. Most of the poems we will consider come from the *Therīgāthā*, a small section of the vast Pali Canon. The *Therīgāthā* has been published twice in English translation by the Pali Text Society, London: first in 1909 (reprinted in 1980) by C. A. F. Rhys Davids in verse under the title *Psalms of the Early Buddhists: The Sisters*; and second in 1971 by K. R. Norman in prose under the title *The Elders' Verses, II*. We have used quotations from both translations here, referring to *Psalms of the Early Buddhists* by page number and to *The Elders' Verses* by verse number. Mrs Rhys Davids' translations have sometimes been slightly modified. Our discussion will also draw upon the verses of bhikkhunis from the Saṁyutta Nikāya (*Kindred Sayings*), included by Mrs Rhys Davids at the end of *Psalms of the Sisters*.

From the poems of the enlightened nuns of the Buddha's time contemporary followers of the Noble Eightfold Path can receive a great deal of instruction, help and encouragement. These verses can assist us in developing morality, concentration and wisdom, the three sections of the path. With their aid we will be able to work more effectively towards eliminating our mental defilements and towards finding lasting peace and happiness.

In some respects, the inspiration from these poems may be stronger for women than for men, since these are in fact women's voices that are speaking. And when the theme of the poem is the mother-child bond, this is bound to be the case. However, at a deeper level the sex of the speakers is irrelevant, for the ultimate truths which they enunciate explain the universal principles of reality which are equally valid for men and for women.

The verses of the nuns, if systematically examined, can help serious Buddhist meditators to understand many central aspects of the Dhamma. The background to the verses, including biographical information on the nuns who uttered them, is provided by the ancient commentary on the *Therīgāthā* by the venerable Ācariya Dhammapāla. Mrs Rhys Davids has included some of these background stories in *Psalms of the Early Buddhists*, and in the first part of this essay we will look at these stories and consider the themes they suggest that are relevant to contemporary students of Buddhist meditation. Then we will go on to discuss a selection of the poems themselves, which deal with many specific teachings of the Buddha.

We of the twentieth century who are seeking to attain liberation will find ourselves deeply grateful to these fully awakened Buddhist nuns of old for their profound assistance in illuminating the Dhamma for us in their own distinctly personal ways.

I
THE BACKGROUND STORIES

The ancient commentaries give us information about each nun's background and also explain the poems themselves. Two major themes of relevance to contemporary students of the Dhamma run through these stories: (1) the immeasurably long time that we have all been lost in *saṁsāra*, the round of birth and death; and (2) the working of the impersonal law of kammic cause and effect which brought these women into contact with the Buddha's teachings in what was to be their final lifetime.

The Long Duration of Saṁsāra

In the original Pali commentaries, the tales of the nuns began many, many rebirths and aeons prior to their final existence at the time of Buddha Gotama. We read how over ages and ages all these women had been living out the results of their old kamma and how they created powerful new kamma based on wisdom, which finally culminated in the attainment of Arahatship, full awakening. Each woman — or, more accurately, each succession of aggregates — had to undergo infinite aeons of suffering in its gross and subtle forms before she was prepared to gain complete insight. But finally she gave up all clinging and was freed from the need ever again to be reborn and suffer, on any plane.

Vipassanā meditators trying to develop this same

understanding of the ultimate nature of conditioned existence can find inspiration if they would apply these tales to their own lives. When we realise how long we ourselves have been wandering in ignorance, constantly generating more and more unwholesome kamma, we will be able to remain patient when our early efforts to train the mind tend to falter or fail. Some of the bhikkhunis who had sufficient *pāramis* — virtues cultivated in previous lives — even to gain Arahatship, still had to put in many years of arduous and sometimes seemingly fruitless effort before they could attain the goal.

For example, Sihā entered the Sangha as a young woman but could not learn to contain her mind's attraction to external objects for seven years. Another nun worked for twenty-five years without finding any substantial peace because of her strong attachment to sense desire. But both these bhikkhunis, when all the appropriate conditions were finally fulfilled, found their patience and continued efforts fully rewarded. So too will we, if we diligently and strictly keep to the Noble Eightfold Path until we become Ariyas, noble ones. Once we have done this, we are assured that we will completely eliminate the causes of all suffering.

By making this effort to live in accordance with the Dhamma and to understand the true nature of existence, we begin to develop strong wholesome mental volitions, kamma that will have effects in future births as well as in this one. The continued efforts in this direction become easier and more natural because, as we wear away ignorance and the other defilements through insight meditation, our minds come to be more strongly conditioned by wisdom *(paññā)*. Recollecting this infinite span of time behind us, and the vast mass of wholesome volitional activities accumulated therein, will help us keep our efforts at purification balanced and strong.

These rebirth stories, illustrating the continuous suffering which every sentient being has undergone during the rounds of *saṁsāra*, can also encourage us to work hard in the Dhamma. Understanding this weighty aspect of the First Noble Truth stimulates us to put forth the great effort required to overcome suffering by penetrating and uprooting its causes, which the Buddha explains are basically craving and ignorance.

Bhikkhuni Sumedhā, in her poem, repeats one of the Buddha's powerful injunctions to eliminate the source of the ceaseless stream of suffering that has rushed on in our previous lives, and will otherwise continue on in the same way throughout the infinite future. Sumedhā is pleading with her parents and fiance to allow her to enter the Sangha rather than force her to marry:

> Journeying-on is long for fools and for those who lament again and again at that which is without beginning and end, at the death of a father, the slaughter of a brother, and their own slaughter.
>
> Remember the tears, the milk, the blood, the journeying-on as being without beginning and end; remember the heap of bones of beings who are journeying-on.

Remember the four oceans compared with the tears, milk and blood; remember the heap of bones (of one man) for one aeon, (as) equal (in size) to Mount Vepula.

(vv. 495-497)

"Journeying-on" is *saṁsāra*. In the lines beginning "Remember the four oceans compared," Sumedhā is reminding her family of a discourse which they must have heard from the Buddha. Each of us, the Buddha tells us, has shed vast oceans of tears over the loss of loved ones and in fear of our own doom as the succession of aggregates has arisen and vanished throughout *saṁsāra's* weary ages. During all these lifetimes, as the verse declares, we have drunk seas and seas of mother's milk, and the blood that was shed when violent death ended our lives also amounts to an immeasurable volume. How could even one gory death be anything but terrible suffering? The Buddha perceived all this with his infinite wisdom and so described it to his followers.

The vastness of *saṁsāra* that we endured before meeting the Dhamma in this life can easily be extrapolated from the stories of these nuns. We must also sustain the patience in our endeavour to wear down ignorance and to develop the awareness of omnipresent suffering which is life in *saṁsāra*, as the First Noble Truth makes known.

Kammic Cause and Effect

The second commentarial theme that can be helpful to us in developing our own understanding of the ultimate nature of reality is the working of the law of kammic cause and effect. None of these nuns was emancipated because one day she decided, "Now I am going to cut off all craving." Nor did the grace of a guru or the power of God or the Buddha himself enlighten them. Rather, it was a very long process in the evolution of the "life continuum" that gradually permitted the conditions for liberation to develop and eventually culminate in Arahatship. Freeing the mind of ignorance, like all activities, is an impersonal cause and effect process. Natural laws of this sort are cultivated and utilized by mental volition to bring about purification. By repeatedly seeing all the phenomena of life as they are by means of concentrated Vipassanā meditation, we gradually wear away the defilements that becloud the mind and cause rebirth with its attendant misery.

For example, Selā took robes when she was a young woman and "worked her way to insight and because of the promise in her and the maturity of her knowledge, crushing the *sankhāras* (conditioned phenomena), she soon won Arahatship" (p. 43). For aeons, Selā had done many good deeds, such as making offerings to and looking after previous Buddhas and their monks. As a result of these meritorious actions over many lifetimes, she was reborn in the heavenly deva planes or in comfortable situations on earth. Eventually, at the time of Buddha Gotama, each of the bhikkhunis, including Selā, came into the Sangha in her own way. Because the time was right for their *pāramis* to bear fruit, all the factors conducive to enlightenment could develop, their defilements could be effaced, and the goal could be achieved.

Sukhā left the world under one of the earlier Buddhas, but she died without becoming an Ariya. Under subsequent Buddhas "she kept the precepts and was learned and proficient in the doctrine." Finally, "in this Buddha era she found faith in the Master at her own home, and became a lay disciple. Later, when she heard Bhikkhuni Dhammadinnā preach, she was thrilled with emotion and renounced the world under her" (pp. 40-41).* All her efforts in past lives then bore their appropriate fruit as Sukhā attained Arahatship and became in turn a great preacher of the Dhamma. Only a small number of nuns are renowned for their skill in teaching, and it is likely that the need to develop the extra *pāramis* to teach the Dhamma made it necessary for Sukhā to study under earlier Buddhas for so long without gaining the paths and fruits.

Similar stories tell of how other bhikkhunis performed good works and put forth effort in previous lives, building various kinds of *pāramis* which allowed them to completely give up all attachment to the world at the time of our Buddha. If we consider the process by which they gradually matured towards liberation, we can see how every mental volition and every deed of body and speech at some time or other bears fruit.

It is due to our own *pāramis*, our own good kamma of the past, that we have the rare and great opportunity to come into contact with the teachings of a Buddha in this lifetime. It is because of wisdom already cultivated that we now have the opportunity

---

* Dhammadinnā will be discussed at greater length below, pp. 46-49.

to develop greater wisdom *(paññāpāramī)* through insight meditation. Wisdom has the power to obliterate the results of past kamma since it comprehends reality correctly. In addition, if we continue to generate such wholesome volitions now, more good kamma is built up which will continue to bear beneficial fruit and bring us closer to the goal.

However, wisdom cannot be cultivated in the absence of morality. The Buddha taught that in order to move towards liberation, it is necessary to keep a minimum of five precepts strictly at all times: abstention from killing, stealing, sexual misconduct, lying and consuming intoxicants. If the precepts are broken, the bad kamma thus created will bring very painful results. Without purity of body and speech, purity of mind cannot be developed as the mind will be too agitated by sense desires, regrets and aversion to settle on its meditation subject properly.

Some of the earlier rebirth stories of Arahat bhikkhunis tell of lives in which they did not keep the precepts. Several of them suffered the results of their unwholesome deeds in animal births or in low forms of human existence. Addhakasī, for example, had a mixed background. She had become a bhikkhuni established in morality under Kassapa Buddha, the Buddha immediately preceding Gotama. But once, due to anger, she referred to a fully liberated senior nun as a prostitute. As a result of that wrong speech, she was reborn in one of the lower realms, for to say or do anything wrong to an Ariya creates worse kamma than to say or do the same thing against a non-Ariya. When the fruit of that bad deed was mostly used up, as a residual effect she herself became a prostitute in her final life. By this time her previous good kamma was the stronger and she ordained as a nun. Keeping the bhikkhuni life pure, Addhakasī attained the goal.

Causes and effects work themselves out and keep the life process going through *saṁsāra*. So long as the mind is attached to anything at all, we will engage in volitional actions, make new kamma, and will have to experience their results. Cultivating good kamma will save one from much suffering and prepare the mind for the most powerful wholesome kamma of all, that born of wisdom, which can eliminate all kammic creation.

II

THE TEACHINGS OF THE POEMS

The actual poems composed by the nuns exhibit a wide range in tone and subject matter. They were almost all spoken after the author had realised that rebirth and all its associated suffering had been brought to an end by the perfection of insight and total elimination of defilements. So virtually all the poems contain some form of "lion's roar," an exclamation that the author has become awakened.

Trivial Incidents Spark Enlightenment

In some cases the poems describe the circumstances which brought the woman into the Sangha or which precipitated her awakening. Both of these can inspire contemporary followers of the Buddha. Sometimes the most mundane event stimulates a ripe mind to see the truth perfectly. Bhikkhuni Dhammā returned from her almsround one day exhausted from heat and exertion. She stumbled, and as she sprawled on the ground a clear perception arose in her of the utter suffering inherent in the body, bringing about total relinquishment. She describes the incident in the following lines:

> Having wandered for alms, leaning on a stick, weak, with trembling limbs I fell to the ground in that very spot, having seen peril in the body. Then my mind was completely released.
> (v. 17)

If someone could gain awakening based on such an event, surely there are an infinite number of potentially enlightening experiences available to all of us for contemplation. Systematic attention *(yoniso manasikāra)* given to any subject will show up its impermanence *(anicca)*, unsatisfactoriness *(dukkha)*, and essenceless nature *(anattā)* and so encourage us to stop craving. However, unless we carefully apply our minds in Vipassanā meditation under the guidance of a competent teacher, it is unlikely that we will be able to utilise our daily encounters with these basic characteristics as means towards liberation. This is because the mind's old conditioning is based on ignorance — the very *inability* to see things as they really are. Only concentrated mindfulness of phenomena in meditation can enable us to comprehend correctly our everyday experiences, because such methodical culture of insight through Vipassanā meditation loosens the old mental tendencies by giving us direct experience of the impermanence of our mind and body.

Entering the Sangha after a Child's Death

Quite a number of women entered the Sangha after their small children had died. Grief is put to good use if it is made the motivation to develop the "path leading to the cessation of suffering." Ubbirī greatly mourned the death of her infant daughter until the Buddha pointed out to her that right in the same charnel ground where she had left this baby's body, she had similarly parted with thousands of children to whom she had given birth in previous lives. Because she had acquired strong merit in the past, this brief personalised discourse was enough to turn Ubbirī from a lamenting mother into an Arahat on the spot. As she clearly saw the vastness of *saṁsāra*, she was prepared to leave it behind. Her profound gratitude to the Buddha is described in these simple lines:

> He has thrust away for me my grief for my daughter. . . . I am without hunger, quenched.
>
> (vv. 51, 53)

With the quenching of ignorance and craving, nothing remains but a pure mind, inherently peaceful. Ubbirī had a pliable, well-prepared mind, and thus she understood, through the Buddha's instructions, that the source of all her suffering had been craving. After countless millions of lifetimes spent rolling in *saṁsāra*, Ubbirī realised how her deep motherly attachment to her children had always caused her much anguish; for sons and daughters, like everything else, are subject to the law of impermanence. We cannot make our loved ones live beyond the span set by their own kamma. This was an insight so powerful for her that no object at all seemed worthy of interest any longer because of the potential pain permeating them all. Thus all tendency to cling was broken, never to reappear.

The life story of Paṭācārā before she came to the Dhamma, described in considerable detail in the commentary to the *Therīgāthā*, is even more dramatic. She lost her entire family, her husband, two small children, parents and brothers in various accidents within a few days. She went insane from the sorrow, but the Buddha's compassion combined with Paṭācārā's *pāramis* from the past enabled her to regain her right mind. When she came into his presence, he taught her to understand how often before she had hopelessly exhausted herself grieving for the dead. She became a Stream-enterer *(sotāpanna)*, one at the first stage of irreversible progress on the path to liberation, and she was ordained. Later, as she was one day pouring water to wash her feet and watching it trickle away — as life does sooner or later for all beings — her mind became utterly free from clinging. Paṭācārā, like Dhammā, had thoroughly developed seeds of understanding, so a very minor mundane incident at just the right moment cleared her mind of every trace of ignorance.

Many other women entered the Sangha in circumstances similar to those of Ubbirī or Paṭācārā. A woman distraught over the death of a child must have been very common in India in those days when limited medical knowledge could not counter a very high infant mortality rate. Therī Paṭācārā spoke to a group of five hundred such grief-stricken mothers, expressing what she had so powerfully learned from similar experience herself:

> The way by which men come we cannot know;
> Nor can we see the path by which they go.
> Why mourn then for him who came to you,
> Lamenting through the tears? . . .
> Weep not, for such is the life of man.
> Unasked he came and unbidden he went.
> Ask yourself again whence came your child

To live on earth this little time?
By one way come and by another gone,
As human to die, and pass to other births —
So hither and so hence — why should you
weep?

(p. 78)

In this way Paṭācārā illustrates for these mothers the natural connection, the invisible, impersonal causal nexus between death and life, life and death. They too took robes and eventually became Arahats. Their joint "lion's roar" culminates in the lines:

Today my heart is healed, my yearning stayed,
Perfected deliverance wrought in me.
I go for refuge to the Buddha, the Sangha
and the Dhamma.

(p. 77)

Because of their physiology and their conditioning by family and society, women are more prone to attachment to their offspring than are men, and so will suffer all the more from their loss. However, if women train their minds to understand how clinging causes enormous suffering, how birth and death are natural processes happening as effects of specific causes, and how infinite the history of such misery is, they can utilise their feminine sufferings in the quest for awakening. In the *Kindred Sayings* (Vol. IV, pp. 62-163), the Buddha himself pointed out the five kinds of suffering unique to women. Three are physiological — menstruation, pregnancy and childbirth. The other two are social, and perhaps not as widely relevant today as they were in ancient Indian society: having to leave her own family to live with her husband and in-laws, and having "to wait upon a man." All five must be the results of past unwholesome deeds, yet each one can be made a basis for insight. Women can train their minds to turn to advantage these apparent disadvantages. They can then make full use of their stronger experiences of the universality and omnipresence of suffering to condition themselves to let go of everything in the conditioned realm.

For some individuals, intense suffering is needed to make the mind relinquish its misconceptions and desires. Paṭācārā is one example of this; Kisā Gotamī is a second. The latter was so unwilling to face the truth of her child's death that she carried the dead baby around with her hoping to find one who could give her medicine to cure him. The Buddha guided her into a realisation of the omnipresence of death by sending her in search of some mustard seed. This is a common ingredient in Indian kitchens, but the Buddha specified that these seeds must come from a household where no one had ever died.

Kisā Gotamī went looking for this "medicine" for her baby, but because of the prevalent joint family system in which three or more generations lived together under one roof, every house she went to had seen death. Gradually, as she wandered through the village, she realised that all who are born must die. Her great *pāramis* then enabled her to understand impermanence so thoroughly that soon afterwards the Buddha confirmed her attainment of Stream-entry. She then spoke these lines:

No village law is this, no city law,
No law for this clan, or for that alone;
For the whole world — and for the gods too —
This is the law: All is impermanent.
(p. 108)

Kisā Gotamī thus transcended the limits of a woman's personal grief to understand one of the basic characteristics of all existence.

Kisā Gotamī later attained Arahatship. Some of the verses she spoke on that occasion give useful lessons to any striver on the Noble Eightfold Path:

Resorting to noble friends, even a fool would be wise. Good men are to be resorted to; thus the wisdom of those who resort to them increases. Resorting to good men one would be released from all pains.

One should know suffering, the cause of suffering and its cessation, and the Eightfold Path; (these are) the Four Noble Truths.
(vv. 213-215)

The company of the wise, especially the guidance of a teacher, is an invaluable help in getting oneself established on the path. But the company of people not involved in the Dhamma will tend to be distracting. Those who are not trying to practise the Buddha's teachings will usually lead us in the worldly direction to which their own minds incline. Thus, when we can, it is best to choose our friends from among meditators.

The Four Noble Truths

As Kisā Gotamī urges in the final lines quoted above, meditators need to train their minds constantly to see the Four Noble Truths in all their ramifications. This is wisdom, *paññā*, the remedy for the ignorance and delusion which are at the root of all suffering as shown in the formula of dependent origination. To develop wisdom one has to ponder these four truths over and over again: (1) the Noble Truth of Suffering *(dukkha)*, which includes all forms of suffering from severe agony to the pervasive unsatisfactoriness and instability inherent in individual existence in all planes of becoming; (2) the Noble Truth of the Cause of Suffering — craving *(taṇhā)*, which drives the mind outwards after sense objects in a state of perpetual unrest; (3) the Noble Truth of the Cessation of Suffering — Nibbāna, which is attained when the causes of suffering, ignorance and craving, have been utterly uprooted; and (4) the Noble Truth of the Way leading to the Cessation of Suffering — the Noble Eightfold Path discovered and taught by the Buddha, consisting in the assiduous practice of morality *(sīla)*, concentration *(samādhi)* and wisdom *(paññā)*.

The Four Noble Truths are concisely expressed in a verse spoken by Mahā Pajāpatī, the Buddha's maternal aunt who brought him up when his own mother, Queen Mahāmāyā, died a week after his birth. It was at the insistence of Mahā Pajāpatī that the Buddha founded the Bhikkhuni Sangha. In her poem she first praises the Buddha for the unique help he has given to so many beings by training them in the way to liberation; then she briefly sums up the Four Noble Truths which she has so thoroughly experienced as ultimate truth. It would be beneficial for modern meditators to consider these lines carefully:

> Now have I understood how ill does come,
> Craving, the Cause, is dried up in me.
> Have I not walked, have I not touched the End
> Of ill — the Ariyan, the Eightfold Noble Path.
> (p. 89)

Buddhist meditators have to train themselves to know these truths as deeply as they can by seeing them in every aspect of existence. We follow the mundane level of the Noble Eightfold Path in order to reach the supramundane *(lokuttara)* path with the attainment of Stream-entry. Then the constituents of the path — morality, concentration and wisdom — are cultivated to the highest degree and the end of suffering, Nibbāna, is realised.

Reaching the Goal after a Long Struggle

When we read the stories of these great bhikkhunis, we see that many of them attained the highest fruits either instantaneously or soon after coming into contact with the Buddha or his Dhamma. This could have happened because they had built up *pāramis* in many previous lives, creating pure kamma of body, speech and mind, while simultaneously wearing out the effects of past kamma.

Yet not all the people whose *pāramis* permitted them to actually hear the Buddha preach were able to become Arahats so quickly in their final lives. When we confront our rebellious minds as we try to follow his path, we can take heart from the tales of nuns who had to put forth years and years of intense persistent effort before they eliminated all their defilements.

A youthful Cittā ordained at her home town of Rājagaha and spent her whole adult life as a nun striving for enlightenment. She finally attained her goal only as a weak old woman, as she laboriously climbed up the landmark of Vultures' Peak. When she had done so, she said:

> Having thrown down my outer robe, and having turned my bowl upside down, I propped myself against a rock, having torn asunder the mass of darkness (of ignorance).
>
> (v. 27)

If we diligently, strictly, and vigorously practise the Noble Eightfold Path, developing insight into the true nature of existence, the opacity of delusion must eventually become completely transparent, cleared by wisdom. It may require many years or many lifetimes of work, but then patience is one of the qualities we must cultivate from the time we first set foot on the path.

Another bhikkhuni who took years to reach enlightenment was Mittākālī. She took robes after hearing the Satipaṭṭhāna Sutta. In her "lion's roar" she describes the errors that cost her seven years to gain Nibbāna. Her poem can be instructive to other meditators both within and outside the Sangha:

> Having gone forth in faith from the house to the houseless state, I wandered here and there,

greedy for gain and honour.

Having missed the highest goal, I pursued the lowest goal. Having gone under the mastery of the defilements, I did not know the goal of the ascetic's state.

(vv. 92-93)

The Buddha pointed out on many occasions that it is dangerous for monks and nuns to pursue gains or favours from the laity, as such activities nullify any attempts they may make to purify their minds. The layman gives gifts to bhikkhus and bhikkhunis to earn merit. If the mind of the recipient is pure, free from greed and other defilements, the merit accruing to the lay disciple is far greater than if the recipient's mind is filled with craving. One of the epithets given to Arahats, whose purity is permanently perfect, is "worthy of the highest offerings." All those, ordained or not, who allow craving to overtake them and waste the precious opportunity they have to practise the Dhamma, will delay their own liberation and increase their suffering.

In the simile of the poisonous snake in the *Middle Length Sayings* (Vol. I, pp. 171-72), the Buddha points out that his teaching has only one aim, freedom from suffering. An incorrect approach that seeks to misuse the Dhamma will lead to increased suffering, just as grasping a snake by the body or tail will result in one's being bitten. The same venomous snake, if grabbed with the help of a forked stick by the neck just behind its head, will safely yield up its poison for medicinal use. The Buddha declares that similarly only those who wisely examine the purpose of his teachings will be able to gain insight and actually experience their purpose — the elimination of the causes of suffering.

When Mittākālī perceived that old age and death were rapidly approaching, she finally came to realise the urgency of the task after wasting years in the pursuit of gain and honour. Since we can never be sure how much longer we will live, it is risky to put off meditation. We have come into contact with the Dhamma under conditions conducive to pursuing the Buddha's goal. Such conditions as youth and human birth will come to an end — either gradually or abruptly — so we can never be certain that the conditions to practise the Dhamma will remain ideal. Mittākālī took years to comprehend that with advancing age, rigidity of mind and bodily ailments were making the job of purification ever more difficult. But once she did realise this, she was able to achieve the goal. Studying this verse of hers may help us to avoid wasting precious time:

> I felt a sense of urgency as I was seated in my little cell; (thinking) "I have entered upon the wrong road; I have come under the mastery of craving.
>
> My life is short. Old age and sickness are destroying it. There is no time for me to be careless before this body is broken."
>
> Looking at the arising and passing away of the elements of existence as they really are, I stood up with my mind completely released. The Buddha's Teaching has been done.
>
> (vv. 94-95)

By observing the rise and fall at every instant of body, feelings, perceptions, mental formations, and consciousness, Mittākālī's mind was freed from misconceptions of any lasting "I" or self. After those seven long years of being trapped in the net of desires, she saw through her foolish and dangerous interest in mundane matters. She was then able to see the elements or aggregates as they actually are: utterly transient *(anicca)*, hence incapable of providing any satisfaction (so *dukkha*), working automatically without any lasting core *(anattā)*. All her worldly involvements dropped away as she attained Arahatship and thenceforth passed beyond all sorrow and suffering.

Perhaps the most moving story of a nun who had to undergo a long struggle from the time she first ordained until she became fully enlightened is that of Punnā. Under six earlier Buddhas, in the vast aeons prior to the Buddha Gotama's dispensation, Punnā was a bhikkhuni "perfect in virtue, and learning the three Pitakas [the Buddhist scriptures] she became very learned in the Norm and a teacher of it. But because of her tendency to pride [each time], she was unable to root out the defilements." Even at the time of Buddha Gotama, she had to work out some bad kamma and so was born as a slave. Hearing one of the Buddha's discourses, she became a Stream-enterer. After she helped her master clear his wrong view, in gratitude he freed her and she ordained. After so many lifetimes of striving, the *pāramis* she had built up as a nun under previous Buddhas ripened. Pride or conceit, always one of the last defilements to go, finally dissolved and she attained Arahatship.

By pondering the accounts of women who attained full awakening after much application and effort, we can be encouraged to continue our own exertions no matter how slow our progress may appear at a given time. In the *Gradual Sayings* (Vol. IV, pp. 83-84), the Buddha gives an analogy of the wearing down of the carpenter's axe handle to illustrate how the mental impurities are to be gradually worn away. Even though the woodcutter cannot say, "This much of the handle was rubbed off today, this much last week," it is clear to him that slowly, over time, the handle is being destroyed. Similarly, a meditator who has a good guide and who constantly attempts to understand the Four Noble Truths and to live in accordance with the Noble Eightfold Path, will gradually eliminate his defilements, even though the steps in the process are imperceptible. Even the Buddha declined to predict the amount of time that will elapse before the final goal is reached. This is conditioned by many interacting factors, such as the good and bad kamma built up in the past and the amount of effort put forth now and in the future. Whether it takes us millions of more lifetimes or a week, we will be sustained in our efforts by the faith that perfection of morality, concentration and wisdom will bring utter detachment and freedom from all suffering.

Liberation means renouncing attachment to oneself and to the world. We cannot rush the process of detachment; insight into the suffering brought about by clinging will do it, slowly. While trying to eliminate mental impurities, we have to accept their existence. We would not be here at all were it not for the ignorance and other defiling tendencies that brought us into this birth. We need to learn to live equanimously with the dirt of the mind while it is slowly being cleared away. Purification, like all other mental activities, is a cause and effect process. Clarity comes slowly with the repeated application of the wisdom of impermanence. If we are patient and cheerfully bear with moments of apparent backsliding or stupidity, if we continue to work energetically with determination, not swerving off the path, the results will begin here and now. And in due time they have to ripen fully.

Contemplation on the Sangha

The Sangha, the order of monks and nuns, preserves and perpetuates the Buddha's pure teachings, and its members have dedicated their lives to practising them. Thus contemplation on the Sangha is recommended by the Buddha to help cultivate wholesome mental states. We could begin such contemplation based on the poem of a bhikkhuni named Rohinī.

Her father had asked her why she thought recluses and monks were great beings. He claimed, as might many people today — particularly in the West with its strong "work ethic" — that ascetics are just lazy; they are "parasites" who do nothing worthwhile and live off the labour of others. But Rohinī proclaimed her faith in the work and lives of pure recluses. She thereby inspired her father's confidence, and at her bidding he then took refuge in the Buddha, the Dhamma, and the Sangha. Her poem can also inspire us:

They are dutiful, not lazy, doers of the best actions; they abandon desire and hatred . . .

They shake off the three roots of evil doing pure actions; all their evil is eliminated . . .

Their body-activity is pure; and their speech-activity is likewise; their mind-activity is pure . . .

They are spotless like mother-of-pearl, purified inside and out; full of good mental states . . .

Having great learning, expert in the doctrine, noble, living in accordance with the doctrine, they teach the goal and the doctrine . . . with intent minds, (they are) possessed of mindfulness . . .

Traveling far, possessed of mindfulness, speaking in moderation, not conceited, they comprehend the end of suffering . . .

If they go from any village, they do not look back (longingly) at anything; they go without longing indeed . . .

They do not deposit their property in a store-room, nor in a pot, nor in a basket, (rather) seeking that which is cooked . . .

They do not take gold, coined or uncoined, or silver; they live by means of whatever turns up . . .

Those who have gone forth are of various families and from various countries; (nevertheless) they are friendly to one another; therefore ascetics are dear to me.

(vv. 275-285)

The Buddhist texts speak of two kinds of Sangha,

both referred to in this poem, the Ariya Sangha and the Bhikkhu Sangha. In the opening lines Rohinī describes the Ariyas, "noble ones," and those striving to attain that state. The three lower kinds of Ariyas may be lay disciples or ordained monks and nuns. But because of their utter purity, the highest type, the fully liberated Arahats, can continue to live only within the Bhikkhu Sangha. It is Arahats who have completely rid their minds of greed, hatred and ignorance, the three roots of evil which Rohinī mentions. Other Ariyas are striving to abandon whatever of these three still remains in their minds. All Ariyas to some extent "comprehend the end of suffering," the Third Noble Truth, for it is this experience of Nibbāna which sets them apart as "noble."

Beginning with the next line, Rohinī specifically talks about the behaviour of monks and nuns. They wander on almsrounds through the streets with their eyes trained just a few steps ahead of them. "They do not look back" as they have no idle interest in the events that are going on around them. They do not handle money and are content with the minimum by way of the requisites — whatever their lay followers may offer them. Students of the Dhamma who are not in the monastic order would also do well to cultivate the monk's lack of interest in his surroundings. A good monk does not let his gaze wander about uncontrolled, especially when he is on almsround, because when going into the village every morning he encounters a plethora of sense objects that might entice him if he does not restrain his senses and maintain mindfulness. Attentively, the good bhikkhu goes silently from door to door and leaves when there is enough food in his bowl, without letting craving disturb his balance of mind. Such a monk is not interested in the details of the lives of those around him. His focus is always on the ultimate nature of things — their impermanence, painfulness and essencelessness. As lay meditators we too need to train ourselves to be like these bhikkhus, to remain equanimous and detached amidst all the clamour and distractions of life by reminding ourselves that none of these things is worth running after.

Rohinī also states that the noble monks are not greedy about money or other possessions. They do not save up their requisites out of fear for the future. Instead, they trust their good kamma to fulfill their daily needs. While, as laymen, we must work for our living, we should heed this behaviour and similarly adopt a detached attitude towards wealth. We work in order to sustain our bodies and those of the people who are dependent on us. But if we can learn to do this without intense longing for the "security" that money seems to provide, we will see how the law of kamma works.

The last verse states that within the Sangha, the family, class or national background of its members does not impede their cordial relations with each other. This kind of open good will is surely useful for laymen to put into practice in their daily lives too. Since it is by ordaining that individuals can completely dedicate their lives to the Dhamma, bhikkhus and bhikkhunis offer us laymen many examples of how we should try to apply the teachings within the limitations of "the dust of household life." Rohinī's poem has pointed out some of these.

The Danger of Worldly Desire

A large number of poems by the nuns emphasize the danger of worldly desire. The bhikkhuni named Sumedhā shaved off her hair herself in order to force her parents to cancel her proposed marriage and permit her to enter the Sangha. But before she left home, Sumedhā convinced her whole family and its retinue of the validity of the Buddha's message. To her fiance, King Anikaratta, she explained the futility of sense desires and the insatiability of the senses:

> Even if the rain-god rained all seven kinds
> Of gems, until earth and heaven were full,
> Still senses would crave and men die unsatiated.
> (p. 176)

No matter how large a quantity of worldly goods we may have, if the mind has not gained insight, craving will recur. If ignorance has not been uprooted, desire will seek more and different objects, always hoping for lasting satisfaction. Durable happiness is impossible in the mundane sphere because all sense objects change and decay every moment, as does the mind itself. This perpetual state of underlying dissatisfaction — craving looking for gratification — is one of the many forms of present suffering. In addition, desire itself generates the kammic energy which propels life towards rebirth in order for it to continue its efforts at finding fulfillment. If desire is present in the mind at the moment of death, rebirth has to ensue.

After speaking the above verse, Sumedhā gave a lengthy discourse to the whole assembly in her palace on the great value of a human birth in the infinity of *saṁsāra*. Life in this world is precious because it provides a very rare opportunity for learning the way to put an end to rebirth and suffering, for putting into practice the teachings of the Buddha. Sumedhā also spoke on the dangers inherent in sensual joy and sense desire and she uttered verses about the Noble Eightfold Path as well. She enthusiastically exhorted her audience:

> When the undying (Nibbāna) exists, what do you want with sensual pleasures which are burning fevers? For all delights in sensual pleasures are on fire, aglow, seething.
>
> (v. 504)

When craving momentarily gains its aim, mind's enjoyment of the sense object brings it to a feverish state of excitement and activity. Sumedhā urges her family to look beyond such unsettling, binding pleasures and to heed the words of the Awakened One which show the way beyond all desire to utter peace. She exhorts them to keep in mind their long-term benefit and not get caught up in the fragile momentary happiness that comes with the occasional satisfaction of sense desire. She reminds them in words we too should recall: "Desires of sense burn those who do not let go" (p. 176). Clinging to pleasure always brings pain. Such agitated emotions, although perhaps pleasant in a gross way, are gone in a moment. They arise and cease due to conditions we cannot completely control. We always tend to want the pleasant to last in spite of the fact that its nature is to change, vanish, and give way to the unpleasant. Sumedhā's poem expounding this wisdom is the last one in the original *Therīgāthā* and it summarizes what the Buddha taught about the dangers of craving.

The bhikkhuni named Subhā also dwells at length on the dangers of mundane wishes, using some terrifying metaphors to show the tremendous dangers inherent in attachment to the world. In the following poem taken from the Saṁyutta Nikāya a meditator can discover much by reflecting on Subhā's intense imagery:

> May I not meet (again) with sensual pleasures, in which no refuge is found. Sensual pleasures are enemies, murderers, like a mass of fire, pain-(ful).
>
> Greed is an obstacle, full of fear, full of annoyance, full of thorns, and it is very disagreeable. It is a great cause of stupefaction . . .
>
> Sensual pleasures are maddening, deceiving, agitating the mind; a net spread out by Māra for the defilement of creatures.
>
> Sensual pleasures have endless perils, they have much pain, they are great poisons, they give little enjoyment, they cause conflict, drying up the virtuous.
>
> (vv. 351f., 357f.)

These lines show us the peril and suffering we must face when we allow ourselves to become entangled in mundane desires. Only personal comprehension of these dangers motivates a meditator to become truly mindful, aware of his physical and mental activities with ever-present detachment. Otherwise his "mindfulness" may be forced, suppressing reactions without helping to untie mental knots. Studying the suffering we have to encounter if we are carried away by our desires, naturally loosens their hold on the mind. We will realise along with Subhā that worldly lusts are enemies and that they herald all the misery of successive births.

One of our tasks in seeking liberation is to train our minds to see desire as it arises at the sense doors. We must also see desire as it persists and as it passes away. Having done this over and over again, we will understand that all desire or attachment is bound to result in unhappiness. In this way we will gradually train our minds to let go of all craving and aversion towards sense objects.

To try to practise this mindfulness without any specific training is likely to fail because the worldling, the average person, perceives no suffering in craving. A worldling can only see the expected happiness. He invariably thinks, "If only this would happen just right, all would be well." But as we purify our bodily and vocal activities through morality, still our minds through concentration, and take up insight meditation under a good teacher, we will come to see more and more clearly how all desire is suffering and brings still more suffering in the future. We will then also realise how often attaining a desired object turns out to be an anti-climax which leaves — not the anticipated happiness — but only emptiness. With a calm mind we can clearly perceive the tension, distress, and uneasiness caused by the continual dissatisfaction, which in turn is due to craving impelling the mind to various sense objects.

Thus the mind is always running — now towards what it foolishly regards as a "desirable" thing, now away from what it considers "undesirable." In Vipassanā meditation, the one-pointed mind is trained to experience directly the transitory nature of body and of mind itself, and also of external sense objects. With this direct knowledge or experiential insight, the "happiness" which is so avidly sought by the worldling is seen as really just another form of suffering, and the perpetual tension caused by the ignorance and craving latent in any unliberated mind becomes evident. As sensual pleasure is understood to be the seething fire described by our bhikkhunis, the mind naturally lets go of all these different manifestations of craving. Such a mind has thoroughly learned the lesson that the nuns gleaned from their Master and passed on to us: suffering is inherent in desire.

The Danger in Attachment to One's Beauty

In ancient times as well as at present, women in all stations of life have used various means to enhance their beauty and to hide the signs of advancing age. This, however, is just a futile attempt to pretend that the body is not growing old, to keep it from showing outwardly that it is actually falling apart. But if, instead of creams and lotions, wisdom is applied to the ageing process, it can deepen our understanding of impermanence on all levels.

Ambapālī was a wealthy and beautiful courtesan during the time of the Buddha. Before she heard the Buddha preach, her main concern had been to cultivate and maintain her renowned beauty. With the Buddha's guidance, she was able to face the inevitability of ageing and the loss of her beauty and to comprehend the suffering of old age. Her verses can also stimulate our own understanding:

> My eyes were shining, very brilliant like jewels, very black and long. Overwhelmed by old age, they do not look beautiful. Not otherwise is the utterance of the speaker of the truth . . .
>
> Formerly my hands looked beautiful, possessing delicate signet rings, decorated with gold. Because of old age they are like onions and radishes. Not otherwise is the utterance of the speaker of the truth . . .
>
> Formerly my body looked beautiful, like a well-polished sheet of gold. (Now) it is covered with very fine wrinkles. Not otherwise is the utterance of the speaker of the truth . . .
>
> Such was this body. (Now) it is decrepit, the abode of many pains, an old house with its plaster fallen off. Not otherwise is the utterance of the speaker of the truth.
>
> (vv. 257, 264, 266, 270)

Ambapālī sees how all the body's charms give way to ugliness and pain as the ageing process takes its toll, as the Buddha teaches it must. All physical beauty, no matter how perfect it might seem at one youthful moment, is utterly impermanent. Even at its peak, the brilliance of the eyes is already, if invisibly, starting to grow dim; the firmness of limbs is withering; the smoothness of skin is wrinkling. Impermanence and decay, Ambapālī reminds us, is the nature of all bodies and of everything else in the universe as well.

Khemā, the queen of King Bimbisāra, was another woman who had been enthralled with her own beauty prior to meeting the Buddha. But Khemā had made a vow before one of the earlier Buddhas to become great in wisdom under the Buddha Gotama. During the dispensations of several of the intervening Buddhas, she had parks made which she donated to each Buddha and his Sangha.

But in her final lifetime Khemā strongly resisted going to see the Buddha Gotama. Perhaps her "Māra forces" were making a last effort to keep her in *saṁsāra*. They were, however, doomed to fail since by the force of her merits this was to be her final existence. King Bimbisāra almost had to trick her into going to the Buddha because Queen Khemā was so attached to her looks and was afraid that this would provoke the Buddha's disapproval. If we ever find ourselves resisting the Dhamma, we can use Khemā's example to remind ourselves of the temporary nature of this mental state. Then we will not take it as a major personal fault. Mind's old habits are not pure, so at times it is bound to struggle against the process of purification.

But the Buddha knew how to tame Khemā's vanity and conceit. He created the vivid image of a woman even more attractive than she was. When she came into his presence, Khemā saw this other lady fanning the Buddha. Then, before the queen's very eyes, the Buddha made the beautiful image grow older and older until she was just a decaying bag of bones. Seeing this, first Khemā realised that her own beauty was not unmatched. This broke her pride. Second and more important, she understood that she herself would likewise have to grow old and decrepit.

The Buddha next spoke a verse and Khemā became a Stream-enterer. Then in rapid succession she went through all the stages of enlightenment to attain Arahatship on the spot. Thereupon the Buddha told King Bimbisāra that she would either have to ordain or to pass away, and the king, unable to bear the thought of losing her so soon, gave her permission to ordain. So, already an Arahat, she was ordained — one of the very rare cases of a human being who had achieved Arahatship before entering the Sangha. Khemā had clearly built up truly unique *pāramis* by giving great gifts to earlier Buddhas and by learning their teachings thoroughly.* Here again we see the great importance of creating in the present strong good kamma based on wisdom, even if we do not attain any of the paths or fruits in this lifetime. The more good deeds accompanied by wisdom that we do now, the easier will it be when the time actually comes for us to reach the goal. Meditation is, of course, the most valuable of such deeds.

In the *Therīgāthā*, Khemā's poem takes the form of a conversation with Māra, the being who controls and symbolises the forces of evil. Māra praised her beauty, and her reply shows how totally her view of herself and of life had changed now that she fully understood the true nature of things:

---

* This story is related in the Commentary to the Dhammapada, translated as *Buddhist Legends* by E. W. Burlingame, published by the Pali Text Society. See Part 3, pp. 225ff.

Through this body vile, foul seat of disease
and corruption,
Loathing I feel, and oppression. Cravings of lust
are uprooted.
Lusts of the body and mind cut like daggers and
javelins.
Speak not to me of delighting in any sensuous
pleasure!
All such vanities cannot delight me any more.
(p. 83)

Then she identifies Māra with those who believe that mere ritual observances will lead to mental purification. Khemā states that such people, who worship fire or the constellations, etc., are ignorant of reality and cannot eliminate their defiling tendencies through such practices. This is why the belief that rites and rituals can bring about liberation has to be eliminated to attain even the stage of Stream-entry.

Khemā concludes her verses with an exclamation of deep gratitude to the Buddha, the supreme among men. Her last line is a resounding "lion's roar":

(I am) utterly free from all sorrow,
A doer of the Buddha's teachings.
(pp. 3 - 4)

Khemā had "done," i.e. put into practice, the message of all the Buddhas, and this had taken her beyond the realms of suffering.

Further Conversations with Māra

Some of the other discourse-type verses in the *Therī-*

gāthā also take the form of a discussion with Māra. Typically, Māra asks the Arahat nun why she is not interested in the "good things of life." Māra urged Selā, for example, to enjoy sensual pleasures while youth allowed her to do so. The therī's reply on the dangers of such delights offers similes as powerful as those used by Bhikkhuni Sumedhā:

> Sensual pleasures are like sword and stakes; the elements of existence are a chopping block for them; what you call 'delight in sensual pleasures' is now 'non-delight' for me.
>
> (v. 58)

Surely many of us have also heard our own internal Māra urge us to "go have a good time and never mind the long-term kammic consequences." But if we can remind ourselves often enough and early enough of the painful after-effects of such "joys" — especially of those that involve breaking moral precepts — we may see through the pleasures of the senses and so gradually lose our attachment to them.

In one of the discourses from the Saṁyutta Nikāya, Calā tells Māra that, unlike most beings, she finds no delight in birth in spite of the so-called sensual pleasures that life makes possible. With clear simplicity she shows that ultimately all that birth produces is suffering:

> Once born we die. Once born we see life's ills —
> The bonds, the torments, and the life cut off.
>
> (p. 186)

We too should cultivate this understanding in order to develop detachment from the poison-soaked sensual pleasures offered by mundane life.

The Doctrine of Anattā

One of the unique aspects of the Buddha's teaching is its doctrine of *anattā*, the impersonal, essenceless, egoless or soul-less nature of all phenomena. This universal characteristic is difficult to comprehend as it is contrary to our most deeply held assumption that "I" exist, that "I" act and "I" feel.

Sakulā, in the following lines of her poem in the *Therīgāthā*, briefly expresses her understanding of the impersonal quality of all compounded things:

> Seeing the constituent elements as other, arisen causally, liable to dissolution, I eliminated all taints. I have become cool, quenched.
>
> (v. 101)

Sakulā has attained Nibbāna because she saw with total clarity that everything normally taken to be "myself" is, in fact, devoid of any such self. She knew that all these phenomena arise and dissolve every moment strictly dependent on causes. This comprehension has rooted out all tendency to cling to the *sankhāras* or "constituent elements" and so all the defiling mental tendencies have ceased.

When Māra asks Sister Selā, "Who made this body, where did it come from and where will it go?", she gives him in reply (in one of the poems added from the Saṁyutta Nikāya) a discourse on egolessness:

Neither self-made the puppet is, nor yet
By another is this evil fashioned.
By reason of a cause it came to be;
By rupture of a cause it dies away.
Like a given seed sown in the field,
Which, when it gets the taste of earth,
And moisture too — by these two does grow,
So the five aggregates, the elements,
And the six spheres of sense — all of these —
By reason of a cause they came to be;
By rupture of the cause they die away.

(pp. 189-190)

After the seed analogy, the last four lines discuss the "self" as it actually is — a compound of conditioned, changing phenomena. The five aggregates make up *nāma* (mentality) and *rūpa* (materiality), each of which is in turn made up of groups of ephemeral factors. *Nāma*, the mental side of existence, consists of the four immaterial aggregates — feeling *(vedanā)*, perception *(saññā)*, mental formations *(sankhārā)*, and consciousness *(viññāṇa)* — which arise together at every moment of experience. *Rūpa*, which may be external matter or the matter of one's own body, consists of the four essential material qualities — solidity, cohesion, temperature, and vibration — along with the derivative types of matter coexisting with them in the very minute material groupings called *kalāpas*, arising and passing away millions of times per second.

Each aggregate arises due to certain causes and when these causes end, the aggregate also ceases. Causes, or conditions, are connected with effects in the law of dependent arising *(paṭiccasamuppāda)*, which is at the centre of the Buddha's own awakening. The refrain from Selā's poem (lines 3-4 and 10-11) is, in fact, a reformulation of the most general exposition of that law often stated thus in the suttas:

When there is this, that comes to be;
With the arising of this, that arises.
When this is absent, that does not come to be;
With the cessation of this, that ceases.

The specific link in the cycle of dependent arising most relevant to Selā's verse is: "With consciousness as condition, mentality-materiality arises." That is, at the moment of conception, *nāma-rūpa* (in this case excluding consciousness) arises due to rebirth-linking consciousness. Later on, during the course of an existence, *nāma*, the mental aggregates, comes into being due to ignorance, past kamma, objects at the sense doors, and many other conditions. *Rūpa*, the matter which makes up the body, arises during life because of food, climate, present state of mind, and past kamma.

Selā also refers to the elements, *dhātu*, a word which the Buddha uses for several groups of phenomena. Let us look here at the eighteen elements. The five sense faculties (eye, ear, nose, tongue, body), their objects (sights, sounds, smells, tastes, touches), and the five types of consciousness dependent on their coming together make up fifteen of the elements. Mind as a faculty, mental objects (ideas), and the mind-consciousness that arises when those two come together are the sixth in each set, completing the eighteen.

The Buddha analysed the totality of conditioned phenomena into ultimate constituents in a number of ways for the benefit of listeners of varying proclivities. To some, the eighteen elements are clear, to others, the five aggregates. Either way, what we need to understand as Selā did is that none of these things is "me" or "mine" or "my self." All these phenomena — the aggregates, the elements, the spheres — arise because of certain conditions, and when those conditions end, naturally they also have to end. When the relevant causes have expended their force, all these aspects of what we erroneously take to be "me" and "mine" cease. So we see with Selā that nowhere is there any real, independent, or lasting "I" with the power to create and sustain itself. There is only the concept "I am" which is conditioned by ignorance, i.e. our inability to see mind-and-body as it really is. The idea "I" is itself essenceless, it arises due to causes; and it is also inherently impermanent, bound to completely disappear when the ignorance and other supporting conditions behind it are uprooted. This is the attainment of Arahatship.

The removal of ignorance takes place step by step in Vipassanā meditation. Every aspect of the mind-body complex comes to be clearly known at its ultimate level as conditioned, essenceless, transitory, oppressive. One comes to fully understand that only when the appropriate conditions come about will a so-called "being" be born. Only then will a five-aggregate life-continuum commence a new life with its bases, elements and sense organs. If we explore Bhikkhuni Selā's seed analogy, we will see in relation to ourselves how a strict succession of causes and effects, kammic and other, governs all of life. We will discover that there is no underlying or ongoing "I" doing or experiencing anything, and will begin to loosen our attachment to this non-existent "self." Then we start to eliminate the dreadful suffering that comes attendant on this delusion.

Suffering follows from the mistaken belief in an "I," technically called *sakkāyadiṭṭhi*, wrong view of a lasting self. On the basis of this idea the mind generates all its thoughts of craving: "I must have this," "I don't like that," "This is mine." It is basically due to this misconception of a controlling self that we have been wandering and suffering throughout aeons in *saṁsāra*. If we are to eliminate all the *dukkha* of existence, as Therī Selā did, we must develop insight through Vipassanā meditation to the point at which understanding of the ultimate truth about mind and body dissolves the mistaken belief in an "I." We can use this bhikkhuni's words to stimulate our own personal meditative experience of the essenceless nature of the five aggregates.

Men and Women in the Dhamma

The difference between the male and female in connection with the Dhamma is a minor theme running through the *Therīgāthā*. It takes two forms: poems whose subject matter is the irrelevance of one's gender for gaining insight, and instances in which a nun specifically inspires or instructs a man with a discourse. The stories of Sumedhā and Rohinī already discussed fit into the latter type.

An example of the first type is Somā's challenge to

Māra's query about women's ability to attain Arahatship. Somā showed Māra that the capacity to gain the requisite insight for liberation need not be hindered by "woman's nature." Somā's encounter with Māra in the *Therīgāthā* proper is explained in her verses from the Saṁyutta Nikāya, where she rhetorically asks him:

> What should the woman's nature do to them
> Whose hearts are firmly set, who ever move
> With growing knowledge onward in the Path?
> (pp. 45; 182-83)

If one is really developing morality, concentration and wisdom, it does not matter whether one was born male or female. The insight to "truly comprehend the Norm" is completely irrespective of superficial distinctions of sex, race, caste, etc. Somā adds that if one even thinks, "Am I a woman in these matters, or am I a man, or what not am I then?" one is under Māra's sway. To be much concerned with such subjects is to remain on the level of conventional truth, clinging to the non-existent self. Repeatedly worrying about which sex is better or about the "inequities" women suffer generates unwholesome kamma. Thoughts like this are rooted in attachment to "I" and "mine" and are associated with ill will or desire.

Moreover, spending time on such matters distracts us from the urgent task of self-purification. Meditators who wish to escape Māra's net need to cast off such thoughts as soon as they are noticed. We should not indulge in or expand upon them. Somā and all the other nuns follow the Buddha's advice closely when they urge us to stick exclusively to the work that will allow us to liberate ourselves from all suffering. All side issues will lose their importance and so pass away with further growth of wisdom. When we know fully that all beings are just impersonal, unstable mind-body processes, generating kamma and feeling its results, our minds will remain with the ultimate truths and have no interest in any conventional concerns.

The story of the bhikkhuni known as "Vaḍḍha's Mother" is one in which a nun specifically guides a man in the Dhamma. This woman joined the Sangha when her son Vaḍḍha was small; thus he had been brought up by relatives. Later, he too ordained and one day went to visit his mother in the bhikkhunis' quarters. On that occasion, she exhorted and inspired him to seek and attain the highest goal:

> Vaḍḍha, may you not have craving for the world at any time. Child, do not be again and again a sharer in pain.
>
> Happily, indeed, Vaḍḍha, dwell the sages, free from lust, with doubts cut off, become cool, having attained self-taming, (being) without taints.
>
> O Vaḍḍha, devote yourself to the way practised by seers for the attainment of insight, for the putting an end to pain.
>
> (vv. 204-205)

From these lines Vaḍḍha deduced that his mother had reached the goal, a fact she confirmed. She again urged him to develop "the path leading to the cessation of suffering" himself. Vaḍḍha, being deeply inspired by his mother's words, also attained the goal and then spoke the following lines praising her:

Truly my mother, because of being sympathetic, applied an excellent goad to me, (namely) verses connected with the highest goal.

Having heard her utterance, the instruction of my mother, I reached a state of religious excitement in the doctrine, for the attainment of rest-from-exertion.

(vv. 210-211)

Here we find a woman's example of perfect sainthood, combined with her timely Dhamma instruction, inspiring a man whose *pāramis* were ripe to put forth the utmost effort and attain complete liberation.

The Five Aggregates and Nibbāna

The Cūlavedalla Sutta (*Middle Length Sayings*, Vol. I) is another sutta in which a bhikkhuni instructs a man. This important text takes the form of a discourse on some fine points of the Dhamma given by the therī Dhammadinnā in reply to questions put to her by her former husband, the lay disciple Visākha. They had been married for some time when he attained the third stage of holiness, that of the Non-returner (*anāgāmi*), by eradicating all traces of ill will and sense desire. Dhammadinnā then learned from him that women too could purify their minds and she obtained his permission to take robes as a nun. By the time of this discussion, she must have already attained Arahatship, the fourth and final stage of holiness.

Visākha first asks Dhammadinnā what the Buddha actually refers to when, using conventional language, he says "own self."* As a Non-returner, Visākha knew the answer to this basic question, but he put it by way of introduction to his progressive series of queries. Dhammadinnā's reply is something for us to ponder. She says that the "five aggregates of grasping" *(pañcupādānakkhandhā)* comprise "own self." She defines the aggregates or groups of grasping as:

the group of grasping after material shape,
the group of grasping after feeling,
the group of grasping after perception,
the group of grasping after habitual tendencies,
the group of grasping after consciousness.

The aggregates are viewed and clung to as myself or mine: this is *sakkāyadiṭṭhi*, the view that there is a lasting self. Actually, there is no lasting controller or core corresponding to the concept "me" or "I." It is merely the grasping after these five groups, which are all that actually makes up "myself," that perpetuates our illusion that there is something substantial. If we can see this, we will be attacking *sakkāyadiṭṭhi* and will come to know that in reality there is no essence, just these five aggregates, all of whose components are continually changing.

The next question Visākha asks Dhammadinnā con-

---

* In Pali, *sakkāya*. I. B. Horner's translation of this term here as "own body" may be misleading. Although the word *kāya* does literally mean "body," it is often used to refer to a collection or assemblage of things, such as a "body of people." Here it signifies the assemblage of psycho-physical phenomena that the worldling identifies as his self.

cerns the reasons for the arising of the aggregates. Quoting the Buddha, she replies that the cause for the aggregates is "craving (that is) connected with again-becoming, accompanied by delight and attachment, finding delight in this and that, namely, the craving for sense pleasures, the craving for becoming, the craving for annihilation."

All craving contributes to the arising of the aggregates over and over again. Being attracted to the things of this world or of the heavenly planes ("craving for sense pleasures") will lead to rebirth there with renewed suffering, gross or subtle. Wanting to keep on going ("craving for becoming") strengthens clinging and ignorance to force us to continue in *saṁsāra*. The belief that there is no form of life after death (rooted in "craving for annihilation") undermines the doctrine of kamma and its result, the understanding of which is essential to moral living.

After a long series of questions and answers which cover the Four Noble Truths, the attainment of cessation, feeling, etc., Visākha asks a final question: "And what, lady, is the counterpart [i.e. equal] of Nibbāna?" Here Dhammadinnā has to stop him:

> This question goes too far, friend Visākha, it is beyond the compass of an answer. Friend Visākha, the Brahmafaring is for immergence in Nibbāna, for going beyond to Nibbāna, for culminating in Nibbāna.

Nothing can possibly be compared with Nibbāna as everything else, be it mental or physical, arises and ceases due to conditions. Nibbāna alone is unconditioned and unchanging. Going beyond the realm of transitory, unsatisfactory phenomena to the utter peace of Nibbāna is the aim of the teaching of the Buddha and so of serious Buddhists. It is useful to keep this goal in mind even during the early stages of meditation, when it may seem remote and vague. The aspiration to attain Nibbāna is cumulative. If it is frequently considered, repeated and combined with the practice of Vipassanā, this aspiration will become a supporting condition for the attainment itself. Frequent recollection of the goal will also keep us from being sidetracked by the pleasurable experiences one may encounter on the path.

After this question and answer session, Dhammadinnā suggests that Visākha should ask the Buddha about all this so that he is certain and learns the answers well. Visākha takes up the idea and later repeats to the Buddha his entire conversation with the therī. The Lord replies in her praise:

> Clever, Visākha, is the nun Dhammadinnā, of great wisdom. . . . If you had asked me, Visākha, about this matter, I too would have answered exactly as the nun Dhammadinnā answered.

Kamma and its Fruit

Finally, let us look at a poem in which a bhikkhuni describes in detail a few of her previous lives and shows her questioner how she comprehended the law of kammic cause and effect working out behind her present-life experiences.

Isidasī had built up many good *pāramis* long ago during the times of former Buddhas. But some seven lifetimes back, when she was a young man, she had committed adultery. After passing away from that existence Isidasī had to suffer the results of this immoral action:

> Therefrom deceasing, long I ripened in Avici hell
> And then found rebirth in the body of an ape.
> Scarce seven days I lived before the great
> Dog-ape, the monkey's chief, castrated me.
> Such was the fruit of my lasciviousness.
> Therefrom deceasing in the woods of Sindh,
> Born the offspring of a one-eyed goat
> And lame, twelve years a gelding, gnawn by worms.
> Unfit, I carried children on my back.
> Such was the fruit of my lasciviousness.
>
> (p. 157)

The next time she was born a calf and was again castrated, and as a bullock pulled a plough and a cart. Then, as the worst of that evil kamma's results had already ripened, Isidasī returned to the human realm. But it was still an uncertain kind of birth as she was the hermaphroditic child of a slave. That life too did not last long. Next, she was the daughter of a man oppressed by debts. One of her father's creditors took her in lieu of payment. She became the wife of that merchant's son, but she "brought discord and enmity within that house."

In her final lifetime, no matter how hard she tried, no home she was sent to as a bride would keep her more than a brief while. Several times her virtuous father had her married to appropriate suitors. She tried to be the perfect wife, but each time she was thrown out. This inability to remain with a husband created an opportunity for her to break through the cycle of results. After her third marriage disintegrated, she decided to enter the Sangha. All her mental defilements were eliminated by meditation, insight into the Four Noble Truths matured, and Isidasī became an Arahat.

She also developed the ability to see her past lives and thus saw how this whole causal chain of unwholesome deeds committed long ago brought their results in her successive existences:

> Fruit of my kamma was it thus that they
> In this last life have slighted me even though
> I waited on them as their humble slave.

The last line of her poem puts the past, rebirth and all its sufferings, completely behind with a "lion's roar": "Enough! Of all that now have I made an end" (p. 163).

In Isidasī's tale we have several instructive illustrations of the inexorable workings of the law of kamma. The suffering she had to undergo because of sexual misconduct lasted through seven difficult lives. But the seeds of wisdom had also been sown and when the force of the bad kamma was used up, the powerful *pāramis* she had created earlier bore their fruit. Hence Isidasī was able to become a bhikkhuni, purify her mind perfectly, and so eliminate all possible causes of future suffering. The beginning, the middle, and the ending of every life are always due to causes and conditions.

* * *

We have now come full circle with these stories of the therīs and have returned to the theme of impersonal causes and effects working themselves out, without any lasting being committing deeds or experiencing results. The infinite sequence of lifetimes steeped in ignorance and suffering is repeated over and over until accumulated *pāramis* and present wisdom, aided by other factors, become sufficiently strong to enable one to see through the craving which has perpetually propelled the succession of aggregates. Through this process these bhikkhunis clearly perceived that their attachments and aversions were the source of all their suffering. Because of this insight, they were able to dissolve the knots of old delusion-based conditioning.

With their completed understanding of suffering, the First Noble Truth, and the abandoning of craving, the Second Noble Truth, their practice of the Noble Eightfold Path, the Fourth Noble Truth, was perfected. They attained the cessation of suffering, the Third Noble Truth, in that very lifetime, and were never reborn again.

The poems of these enlightened nuns, telling how they came to meet the Buddha, how they had built up wisdom and other meritorious kamma over many previous lives, how they understood the Buddha's teachings, and how they attained Arahatship, offer us inspiration and guidance. They can help us present-day Buddhists to practise Vipassanā meditation and to gain insight into suffering and its causes. Then we too will be able to give up all craving by developing wisdom. We can use the messages of the therīs to assist us in putting an end to our own suffering.

Grateful for their assistance, may we all follow in the footsteps of these great nuns, true daughters of the Buddha. May our minds be perfect in wisdom, perfectly pure, and utterly free from all possibility of future suffering.

ABOUT THE AUTHOR

Susan Elbaum Jootla was born in New York City in 1945 and obtained B.A. and M.A. degrees in Library Science from the University of Michigan. She is married to an Indian, Balbir S. Jootla, with whom she lives in the Western Himalayan hill station of Dalhousie. They have both been practising Vipassanā meditation in the tradition of the late Sayagyi U Ba Khin of Burma since 1970 and are now students of his leading disciple, Mother Sayama, who directs the International Meditation Centres in England and Rangoon. Her previous BPS publications are "Right Livelihood: The Noble Eightfold Path in the Working Life" in *The Buddhist Layman* (Wheel No. 294/295) and *Investigation for Insight* (Wheel No. 301/302). Her book *Buddhism in Practice*, about the meditation tradition of U Ba Khin, is scheduled for publication by Motilal Banarsidass of India.

Recommended for further reading

Women in Early Buddhist Literature
I. B. Horner (Wheel No. 30)

Stories of Old
Translations from the Pali Commentaries by
Theras Nyanamoli & Nyaṇaponika
(Wheel No. 59)

With Robes and Bowl
On the wandering ascetic monks of Thailand
Bhikkhu Khantipalo (Wheel No. 83/84)

The Message of the Saints
Essay on the Thera- & Therīgāthās
V. F. Gunaratna (Wheel No. 135)

The Position of Women in Buddhism
Dr. Mrs. L. S. Dewaraja (Wheel No. 280)

Buddhist Women at the Time of the Buddha
Hellmuth Hecker (Wheel No. 292/293)

Banner of the Arahants
The story of Buddhist monks and nuns from the Buddha's time till now
Bhikkhu Khantipalo

Lives of the Great Buddhist Disciples

Life of Sāriputta by Nyanaponika Thera (Wheel No. 90/92). Sariputta was the Buddha's foremost disciple, the most distinguished in wisdom and a man of the highest saintly qualities. This full biographical study examines the man and his teaching, vividly demonstrating why Sāriputta is held in such high veneration throughout the Buddhist world.

Life of Mahā Moggallāna by Hellmuth Hecker (Wheel No. 115). A biography of the Buddha's second chief disciple, who excelled in supernormal knowledge and in psychic powers.

Life of Ananda by Hellmuth Hecker (Wheel No. 273/274). Ananda was the personal attendant of the Buddha and the most learned of the great disciples. His prodigious memory enabled him to serve as the "guardian of the Dhamma," a role through which he could ensure the continued transmission of the Dhamma to the world.

Life of Angulimāla by Hellmuth Hecker (Wheel No. 312). The moving story of a notorious criminal, the murderer of almost a thousand people, who was transformed by the Buddha into an enlightened and liberated man.

Anāthapindika the Great Benefactor by Hellmuth Hecker (Wheel No. 334). A biography of the chief lay disciple of the Buddha, a multi-millionaire who was also a man of deep spiritual insight and vast compassion, whose very name means "feeder of the poor."

Mahā Kassapa: Father of the Sangha by Hellmuth Hecker (Wheel No. 345). A biographical survey of the great disciple whose spiritual depth and natural authority elevated him to a position of leadership within the Sangha in the period following the passing away of the Buddha.

THE BUDDHIST PUBLICATION SOCIETY

is an approved charity dedicated to making known the Teaching of the Buddha, which has a vital message for people of all creeds.

Founded in 1958, the BPS has published a wide variety of books and booklets covering a great range of topics. Its publications include accurate annotated translations of the Buddha's discourses, standard reference works, as well as original contemporary expositions of Buddhist thought and practice. These works present Buddhism as it truly is — a dynamic force which has influenced receptive minds for the past two thousand years and is still as relevant today as it was when it first arose.

A full list of our publications will be sent free of charge upon request. Write to:

The Hony. Secretary
BUDDHIST PUBLICATION SOCIETY
P.O. Box 61
54, Sangharaja Mawatha
Kandy Sri Lanka